LET THE

NATIONS

BE GLAD!

DVD STUDY GUIDE

LET THE
NATIONS
BE GLAD!

DVD STUDY GUIDE

JOHN PIPER

DEVELOPED BY DESIRING GOD

Baker Academic
a division of Baker Publishing Group
Grand Rapids, Michigan

Published by Baker Academic
a division of Baker Publishing Group
P.O. Box 6287, Grand Rapids, MI 49516-6287
www.bakeracademic.com

Printed in the United States of America

ISBN 978-0-8010-3642-2

10   11   12   13   14   15   16   7   6   5   4   3   2   1

Contents

Introduction to This Study Guide

Our future hope as Christians has been painted for us in the brush strokes of Revelation. The canvas depicts a day when there will be an ocean of people before the throne of God thundering songs of endless praise: "Worthy is the Lamb who was slain, to receive power and wealth and wisdom and might and honor and glory and blessing!" (Rev. 5:12). The Lord is pursuing this great end. This is the very heart of God. "Let the peoples praise you, O God; let all the peoples praise you! Let the nations be glad and sing for joy, for you judge the peoples with equity and guide the nations upon earth. Selah. Let the peoples praise you, O God; let all the peoples praise you!" (Ps. 67:3–5).

World missions must not merely be another line item in the church budget. The Bible places far too much emphasis on it for that. As the people of God, we are called to be zealous for the *peoples* of God: the tribes and tongues and languages and nations that he has bought with the blood of his Son. As disciples of Christ, we must make it our ambition to make disciples of all nations, baptizing them in the name of the Father and the Son and the Holy Spirit. This is the passion of the Lord; that *all* the peoples praise him. The stakes are high and the cost is great, but the joy is greater.

The aim of this study guide is that your heart's worship would be fueled from a flame to an inferno while you grow in understanding of the fervor that God has for the peoples of the earth: from the Bedouin to the Pashtun, the Somali to the Sunda, the Japanese to the Bhutanese. We do not want the American dream to be your spiritual suicide. The comforts of the culture are ready to strangle the vitality that would make your heart beat healthier and stronger. John Piper has given the ultimatum for every Christian: "When it comes to world missions, there are only three kinds of Christians: zealous goers, zealous senders, and disobedient."[1] Our hope is that after you have finished this study guide you will enthusiastically fall under either of the first two categories. We desire that your capacities for joy will be enlarged in seeing God's global redemptive purposes in his own end for which he created the world.

This study guide is designed to be used in an eight-session[2] guided group study that focuses on *Let the Nations Be Glad!* DVD Set.[3] After an introductory lesson, each subsequent lesson examines one 30-minute session[4] from *Let the Nations Be Glad!* DVD Set. You, the learner, are encouraged to prepare for the viewing of each DVD session by reading and reflecting upon Scripture, by considering key quotations, and by asking yourself penetrating questions. Your preparatory work for each lesson is marked with the heading "Before You Watch the DVD, Study and Prepare" in Lessons 2–7.

The workload is conveniently divided into five daily (and manageable) assignments. There is also a section suggesting further study (see below). This work is to be completed individually before the group convenes to view the DVD and discuss the material.

> Throughout this study guide, paragraphs printed in a shaded box (like this one) are excerpts from a book written by John Piper, or excerpts taken from the Desiring God website. They are included to supplement the study questions and to summarize key or provocative points.

---

1. John Piper, "A Passion for the Supremacy of Christ—Where He Is Not Named," an online sermon at www.DesiringGod.org.

2. While this study guide is ideally suited for an eight-session study, it is possible to complete it in six sessions. The Leader's Guide at the end of this study guide contains a suggestion on one way to complete this study in six weeks. The six-session option may be well-suited for groups that are already familiar with each other or that only have six weeks to complete the study.

3. Although this resource is designed to be used in a group setting, it can also be used by the independent learner. Such learners would have to decide for themselves how to use this resource in the most beneficial way. We would suggest doing everything but the group discussion, if possible.

4. Thirty minutes is only an approximation. Some sessions are longer; others are shorter.

The second section in Lessons 2–7, entitled "Further Up and Further In," is designed for the learner who wants to explore the concepts and ideas introduced in the lesson in greater detail. This section is not required but will deepen your understanding of the material. This section requires that you read online sermons or articles from the Desiring God website, www.DesiringGod.org, and answer relevant questions. These sermons can be found by performing a title search at the Desiring God website.

The third section in Lessons 2–7, entitled "While You Watch the DVD, Take Notes," is to be completed as the DVD is playing. This section includes fill-in-the-blanks and leaves space for note-taking. You are encouraged to engage with the DVD by filling in the appropriate blanks and writing down other notes that will aid you in the group discussion.

The fourth section in each normal lesson is "After You Watch the DVD, Discuss What You've Learned." Three discussion questions are provided to guide and focus the conversation. You may record, in the spaces provided here, notes that will help you contribute to the conversation. Or, you may use this space to record things from the discussion that you want to remember.

The fifth and final section is an application section: "After You Discuss, Make Application." You will be challenged to record a "take-away point" and to engage in a certain activity that is a fitting response to the content presented in the lesson.

Group leaders will want to find the Leader's Guide, included at the end of this study guide, immediately.

Life transformation will only occur by the grace of God. Therefore, we highly encourage you to seek the Lord in prayer throughout the learning process. Pray that God would open your eyes to see wonderful things in his Word. Pray that he would grant you the insight and concentration you need in order to get the most from this resource. Pray that God would cause you to not merely understand the truth but also to rejoice in it. And pray that the discussion in your group would be mutually encouraging and edifying. We've included objectives at the beginning of each lesson. These objectives won't be realized without the gracious work of God through prayer.

Introduction to
Let the Nations Be Glad!

Lesson Objectives

It is our prayer that after you have finished this lesson . . .

- You will hear how others in your group approach the subject of missions.
- Your curiosity will be aroused and questions will come to mind.
- The Lord will begin to enlarge your heart for greater capacities of joy because of his desires for all peoples.

About Yourself

1. What is your name?

2. Tell the group something about yourself that they probably don't already know.

3. Briefly explain why you are participating in this study.

A Preview of *Let the Nations Be Glad!*

1. Tell the group what you know about missions. What do Christians mean when they say "missions"? Is missions foreign, domestic, or both? Must it be cross-cultural? How does missions relate to other important tasks like evangelism, church-planting, and Bible translation?

2. Do you believe the Bible is concerned with missions? If so, why is it? Do you believe the Bible speaks extensively about missions or is it just limited to particular New Testament texts? If possible, use Scripture to support your answer.

Lesson 2

Defining Missions and Defining Peoples

Lesson Objectives

It is our prayer that after you have finished this lesson . . .

- You will have a better grasp on what biblical missions is.
- You will have a better grasp on defining peoples and nations.
- Your heart will begin to see the depth of God's concern for the nations.

Before You Watch the DVD, Study and Prepare

Day 1—Defining Missions

Before beginning this study, we will do well to clarify certain common terms. Many arguments and debates would be settled more quickly if each party involved in the discussion were to clearly define their terms. This particular discussion on missions is no exception.

13

Question 1: Write down in your own words a clear definition of "missions" using biblical texts as your support.

Question 2: Interact with the following statement: "All Christians are missionaries." Is this true or false? Should we make distinctions between foreign or cross-cultural missions and domestic ministry? Explain your answer and, if possible, incorporate biblical passages.

Day 2—Defining Peoples

Even after defining "missions" and the differences between frontier work and domestic evangelism, more clarifications must be made in regard to what qualifies as frontier missions. Is it geographical, ethnic, political, or linguistic? It is important that we derive our definitions from the Bible and not impose our own notions on it.

Look at Matthew 24:14; Revelation 5:9; and Genesis 12:2–3.

Matthew 24:14
And this gospel of the kingdom will be proclaimed throughout the whole world as a testimony to all nations, and then the end will come.

Revelation 5:9
And they sang a new song, saying, "Worthy are you to take the scroll and to open its seals, for you were slain, and by your blood

you ransomed people for God from every tribe and language and people and nation.

Genesis 12:2–3 .

And I will make of you a great nation, and I will bless you and make your name great, so that you will be a blessing. I will bless those who bless you, and him who dishonors you I will curse, and in you all the families of the earth shall be blessed.

Question 3: What do you think each of these passages means by "nations" or "families of the earth"? How do these texts help to illuminate each other?

> What we have found, in fact, is that a precise definition is probably not possible to give on the basis of what God has chosen to reveal in the Bible. God probably did not intend for us to use a precise definition of people groups. That way we can never stop doing pioneer missionary work just because we conclude that all the groups with our definition have been reached.
>
> For example, the point of Matthew 24:14 . . . is not that we should reach all the nations as we understand them and then stop. The point rather is that as long as the Lord has not returned, there must be more people groups to reach, and we should keep on reaching them.[1]

The hope at this point is that you begin to feel the difficulty in precisely defining the parameters of a people group. The Bible has not given us these clear-cut distinctions.

Missiologists often distinguish between "reached" people groups and "unreached" people groups. Moreover, the same could be said concerning "unreached" and "reached" people groups.

---

1. John Piper, *Let the Nations Be Glad!* 3rd ed. (Grand Rapids: Baker Academic, 2010), 212.

Question 4: What do you think is meant by these two classifications? How would you determine if a people group has been "reached"?

There is a difficulty with defining the specific task of missions as planting an indigenous church in every people group. The difficulty is that our *biblical* definition of people groups may be so small and so closely related to another group that such a church would be unnecessary. How large was the family or clan of Carmi in the tribe of Reuben, or the family of Achan in the tribe of Judah? And are we sure that the families in Genesis 12:3 are so distinct that each must have its own church? When Paul said that his special missionary work was completed from Jerusalem to Illyricum, had he in fact planted a church in every family or clan?[2]

These questions show that there will always be some ambiguity in the definition of "reached" and in the aim of missionary work.

Day 3—Our Suffering and Our Song

Jesus promises a hard life for those who believe in him and follow him. But the Bible also gives promises of everlasting life and joy in the Lord.

Examine John 12:24–25; Matthew 16:24–25; Proverbs 4:18; and Psalm 96:1.

John 12:24–25

Truly, truly, I say to you, unless a grain of wheat falls into the earth and dies, it remains alone; but if it dies, it bears much

---

2. Ibid., 217–18.

fruit. Whoever loves his life loses it, and whoever hates his life in this world will keep it for eternal life.

Matthew 16:24–25
Then Jesus told his disciples, "If anyone would come after me, let him deny himself and take up his cross and follow me. For whoever would save his life will lose it, but whoever loses his life for my sake will find it."

Proverbs 4:18
But the path of the righteous is like the light of dawn, which shines brighter and brighter until full day.

Psalm 96:1
Oh sing to the LORD a new song; sing to the LORD, all the earth!

Question 5: What are the marks of the Christian life according to these verses? How can the Christian who hates his life at the same time be joyfully singing? Explain this seeming inconsistency.

Suppose a believer who was on his deathbed said to his friends in his last few moments alive, "Don't worry. Don't you know that my death is my gain because I'm going to be with Christ?"

Question 6: What would such a statement communicate about the worth of Christ? In light of the passages you examined for Question 5, how might such a testimony relate to gospel proclamation?

It is simply amazing how consistent are the testimonies of missionaries who have suffered for the gospel. Virtually all of them bear witness to the abundant joy and overriding compensations (a hundredfold!).

Andrew Murray refers to this "law of life" in his missionary classic, *Key to the Missionary Problem*. Nature teaches us that every believer should be a soul-winner: "It is an essential part of the new nature. We see it in every childe who wants to tell of his happiness and to bring others to share his joys." Missions is the automatic outflow and overflow of love for Christ. We delight to enlarge our joy in Him by extending it to others.[3]

Day 4—The Global Heart Is the Healthy Heart

There are certain implications in having a heart that is on board with God's global purposes and his work in history. J. Campbell Wright reflects upon some of the effects for the Christian.

Most men are not satisfied with the permanent output of their lives. Nothing can wholly satisfy the life of Christ within the life of his followers, except the adoption of Christ's purpose toward the world that he came to redeem. Fame, pleasure, riches, are but husks and ashes in contrast with the boundless and abiding joy of working with God for the fulfillment of his eternal plans. The men who are putting everything into Christ's global undertaking are getting out of life its sweetest and most priceless rewards.[4]

Question 7: Given J. Campbell Wright's observation, what are the effects on the Christian heart if there is no concern for missions? What are the effects on the church?

---

3. John Piper, *Desiring God* (Sisters, Ore.: Multnomah, 2003), 245.

4. J. Campbell Wright, as quoted by John Piper in *Don't Waste Your Life* (Wheaton: Crossway Books, 2003), 170.

John Piper also explains the effects on the Christian heart in having a global vision of the gospel.

> We will not know God in his full majesty until we know him moving triumphantly among the nations. We will not admire and praise him as we ought until we see him gathering a company of worshipers for himself from every people group on earth—including all the Muslim and Hindu and Buddhist peoples. Nothing enlarges our vision of God's triumphant grace like the scope of his saving work in history.[5]

Question 8: Articulate the reason why a heart grows healthier the more it is concerned with global missions. In other words, why will we not admire and praise God as we ought until we embrace God's global work?

Day 5—One Purpose-Driven Mission

The apostle Paul was perhaps the most effective and fruitful missionary in history. In the book of Romans, Paul articulates the purpose of his mission.

Reflect on Romans 1:5 and 15:8–12.

Romans 1:5
[Jesus Christ] . . . through whom we have received grace and apostleship to bring about the obedience of faith for the sake of his name among all the nations.

Romans 15:8–12
For I tell you that Christ became a servant to the circumcised to show God's truthfulness, in order to confirm the promises given to the patriarchs, and in order that the Gentiles might glorify God for his mercy. As it is written, "Therefore I will praise you

---

5. Piper, *Don't Waste Your Life*, 172–73.

among the Gentiles, and sing to your name." And again it is said, "Rejoice, O Gentiles, with his people." And again, "Praise the Lord, all you Gentiles, and let all the peoples extol him." And again Isaiah says, "The root of Jesse will come, even he who arises to rule the Gentiles; in him will the Gentiles hope."

John Piper comments on Romans 15:8–12 regarding the use of "Gentiles."

> Paul gathers four Old Testament quotations about the *ethnē*, all of which in their Old Testament context refer to nations, not just to Gentile individuals.[6]

Question 9: Underline each use of the words "nations" or "Gentiles." Then, using a cross-reference tool like those found in the margins of many Bibles, locate each Old Testament quotation and write them down.

Question 10: Read the context for each of the Old Testament quotes noted in the last question. Write down any observations regarding similarities between each of them. What statement is Paul supporting in Romans by quoting these Old Testament texts?

Further Up and Further In

Note: The "Further Up and Further In" section is for those who want to study more. It is a section for further reference and going deeper. The phrase "further up and further in" is borrowed from C. S. Lewis.

As noted in the introduction, each lesson in this study guide provides the opportunity for you to do further study. In this section, you will

---

6. Piper, *Let the Nations Be Glad!* 201.

have the opportunity to read a sermon or article and answer some questions about what you read.

Read "Unreached Peoples," an online article at www.DesiringGod .org.

Question 11: In your own words, write down the question that is posed in the first section. What is the point in using the illustration described in this section?

Meditate on Matthew 28:19.

Matthew 28:19
Go therefore and make disciples of all nations, baptizing them in the name of the Father and of the Son and of the Holy Spirit.

Question 12: John Piper presents two alternative interpretations for "all nations" (*panta ta ethnē*). Restate the two different interpretations in your own words and then use other Scriptures to support the interpretation that *panta ta ethnē* in Matthew 28:19 means "all nations" or "all people groups."

Study John 10:16 and 11:49–52.

John 10:16
And I have other sheep that are not of this fold. I must bring them also, and they will listen to my voice. So there will be one flock, one shepherd.

John 11:49–52
But one of them, Caiaphas, who was high priest that year, said to them, "You know nothing at all. Nor do you understand that it is better for you that one man should die for the people, not that

the whole nation should perish." He did not say this of his own accord, but being high priest that year he prophesied that Jesus would die for the nation, and not for the nation only, but also to gather into one the children of God who are scattered abroad.

Question 13: Underline every reference to nations or peoples. How does what Caiaphas says relate to the atonement? What is the purpose mentioned in Caiaphas's prophecy?

It's no wonder why many Calvinists throughout church history have been the most active in mission efforts. The Doctrines of Grace have given missionaries confidence in their mission. Particularly, the doctrine of limited atonement has been a ballast in the boat of frustrated missionaries. John Piper defines limited atonement below.

> The term "limited atonement" addresses the question, "For whom did Christ die?" But behind the question of the extent of the atonement lies the equally important question about the nature of the atonement.
>
> The Arminian limits the nature and value and effectiveness of the atonement so that he can say that it was accomplished even for those who die in unbelief and are condemned. In order to say that Christ died for all men in the same way, the Arminian must limit the atonement to a powerless opportunity for men to save themselves from their terrible plight of depravity.
>
> On the other hand we do not limit the power and effectiveness of the atonement. We simply say that in the cross God had in view the actual redemption of his children. And we affirm that when Christ died for these, he did not just create the opportunity for them to save themselves, but really purchased for them all that was necessary to get them saved, including the grace of regeneration and the gift of faith.[7]

---

7. John Piper, "What We Believe about the Five Points of Calvinism," an online article at www.DesiringGod.org.

Reflect on Revelation 5:9–10.

Revelation 5:9–10
And they sang a new song, saying, "Worthy are you to take the scroll and to open its seals, for you were slain, and by your blood you ransomed people for God from every tribe and language and people and nation, and you have made them a kingdom and priests to our God, and they shall reign on the earth."

Question 14: Explain why Revelation 5:9–10 would be a powerful doctrinal statement in regards to particular redemption or limited atonement given the definition laid out above.

Read Revelation 7:9–10; 14:6–7; 15:4; and 21:3.

Revelation 7:9–10
After this I looked, and behold, a great multitude that no one could number, from every nation, from all tribes and peoples and languages, standing before the throne and before the Lamb, clothed in white robes, with palm branches in their hands, and crying out with a loud voice, "Salvation belongs to our God who sits on the throne, and to the Lamb!"

Revelation 14:6–7
Then I saw another angel flying directly overhead, with an eternal gospel to proclaim to those who dwell on earth, to every nation and tribe and language and people. And he said with a loud voice, "Fear God and give him glory, because the hour of his judgment has come, and worship him who made heaven and earth, the sea and the springs of water."

Revelation 15:4
Who will not fear, O Lord, and glorify your name? For you alone are holy. All nations will come and worship you, for your righteous acts have been revealed.

Revelation 21:3
And I heard a loud voice from the throne saying, "Behold, the dwelling place of God is with man. He will dwell with them, and they will be his people, and God himself will be with them as their God."

Question 15: Underline every reference to nations or peoples. What is one of the main purposes of God in the book of Revelation according to these passages? Write down any other observations.

While You Watch the DVD, Take Notes

What does John Piper say is the thesis of these talks?

What are the five different aims John Piper has in these talks?

One of the great tragedies of American responses to this new situation is the conclusion that . . .

List the four questions that John Piper will be addressing in the coming sessions.

The task of missions is not defined uniquely by _____ the number of people who get saved. If this were true, you would just find the most _____ _____ and then stay there forever. . . . Missions thinks you keep crossing _____ and _____ until all the peoples have a strong _____ and experience the focus of local missional living.

After You Watch the DVD, Discuss What You've Learned

1. Interact with the following statement: "We Americans don't need to send missionaries to Bhutan. Wouldn't it seem more financially responsible and culturally effective to find and support someone who is culturally closer to the Bhutanese than we are? The surrounding peoples in India are far more likely to reach them than we are." Discuss why this argument may not necessarily be true.

2. Discuss the relationship between a heart that is content and full of joy in the Lord (Phil. 1:21) and the mission task. What impact does a discontented person have on his mission?

3. Define *missions* in light of what you've learned in this lesson. Why should *missions* not be considered maximizing the number of individuals saved? Use the biblical texts you have heard in this lesson to support your answer.

After You Discuss, Make Application

1. What was the most meaningful part of this lesson for you? Was there a sentence, concept, or idea that really struck you? Why? Record your thoughts in the space below.

2. Using the Joshua Project website (www.joshuaproject.net), choose one unreached people group and commit to pray for that group every day throughout this study.

The Urgency of Missions

The Reality of Hell and the Work of Christ

Lesson Objectives

It is our prayer that after you have finished this lesson . . .

- You will see God's desire for the nations in the Abrahamic covenant.
- You will better understand the distinction between local evangelism and Pauline missions.
- You will be able to articulate the importance that the doctrine of eternal hell has for pioneer missions.

Before You Watch the DVD, Study and Prepare

Day 1—The Extension of the Abrahamic Covenant

The mission task was never limited to the Great Commission. There are plenty of Old Testament references that testify to this endeavor. The whole Bible testifies to missions because our God is a missionary God.

Examine Genesis 12:1–3.

27

Genesis 12:1–3

Now the LORD *said to Abram, "Go from your country and your kindred and your father's house to the land that I will show you. And I will make of you a great nation, and I will bless you and make your name great, so that you will be a blessing. I will bless those who bless you, and him who dishonors you I will curse, and in you all the families of the earth shall be blessed."*

Question 1: What does God promise Abram? What is the purpose for God's covenant with him? To whom is the blessing of Abraham extended?

Now look at Genesis 17:4–5 and Paul's understanding of the Abrahamic covenant in Romans 4:16 and Galatians 3:16.

Genesis 17:4–5

Behold, my covenant is with you, and you shall be the father of a multitude of nations. No longer shall your name be called Abram, but your name shall be Abraham, for I have made you the father of a multitude of nations.

Question 2: What does God promise Abraham in this passage? What is a natural understanding of the phrase "multitude of nations" in this passage?

Day 2—The Abrahamic Covenant and the Psalms

One natural way to understand the promise to Abraham is that he will be the father of all those who trace their genealogy back to him. Thus, ethnic Jews and Arabs could trace their lineage back to Abraham (through Isaac and Ishmael, respectively).

Study Romans 4:16 and Galatians 3:16.

Romans 4:16
That is why it depends on faith, in order that the promise may rest on grace and be guaranteed to all his offspring—not only to the adherent of the law but also to the one who shares the faith of Abraham, who is the father of us all.

Galatians 3:16
Now the promises were made to Abraham and to his offspring. It does not say, "And to offsprings," referring to many, but referring to one, "And to your offspring," who is Christ.

Question 3: How does Paul understand the promise to Abraham? Does it only extend to those who are biologically descended from Abraham? Underline the key phrase.

Paul thinks sonship does not depend on physical descent. For example, in Galatians 3:28–29 he says, "There is neither Jew nor Greek, there is neither slave nor free, there is neither male nor female, for you are all one in Christ Jesus. And if you are Christ's, then you are Abraham's offspring, heirs according to the promise." So the first thing to be said is that Jews and non-Jews can be offspring or children or sons of Abraham. Sonship does not depend on physical descent.

I know it sounds strange to us, but it is very close to the heart of the gospel: white Anglo-Saxon protestants can become sons of Abraham; Hispanics and Laotians and Cambodians can become sons of Abraham; black African Muslims can become sons of Abraham; anti-Semitic, redneck Nazi vigilantes can become sons of Abraham; Hitler could have become a son of Abraham.[1]

---

1. John Piper, "Those Who Have Faith Are the Sons of Abraham," an online sermon at www.DesiringGod.org.

The global purposes of God are not only found within the Genesis account of God's covenant with Abraham. The Psalms ring with calls for the nations to worship the God of Israel. Examine the following passages.

Psalm 47:1
Clap your hands, all peoples! Shout to God with loud songs of joy!

Psalm 72:11
May all kings fall down before him, all nations serve him!

Psalm 86:9
All the nations you have made shall come and worship before you, O Lord, and shall glorify your name.

Psalm 96:7
Ascribe to the LORD, O families of the peoples, ascribe to the LORD glory and strength!

Question 4: These verses are isolated statements, but the call for global worship is pervasive throughout all 150 chapters of Psalms. Articulate the connection between the passionate affection for God expressed in the Psalms, the command to glorify him, and the call to the nations.

This missionary impulse to all the nations is flowing from singing and calling for singing. "Oh sing to the Lord a new song; sing to the Lord, all the earth!" This is a singing mission. This is the way you feel when your team has won the Super Bowl or the World Cup or the cross-town rivalry—only a thousand times greater. "Declare his glory among the nations, his marvelous works among all the peoples!" We are speaking of glory. We are speaking of

> marvelous works, not boring works. Nor ordinary works.
> We have tasted and seen that this God is greater to know
> than all other greatness. "Great is the Lord, and greatly
> to be praised" (v. 4). We are exhilarated to know him and
> sing to him and call the world to sing with us to him.[2]

Day 3—I Have Fulfilled the Gospel

Toward the end of the book of Romans, Paul makes an audacious statement regarding his mission and accomplishments. This text has great implications for how we understand the distinction between local evangelism and frontier missions.

Examine Romans 15:17–21.

Romans 15:17–21

In Christ Jesus, then, I have reason to be proud of my work for God. For I will not venture to speak of anything except what Christ has accomplished through me to bring the Gentiles to obedience—by word and deed, by the power of signs and wonders, by the power of the Spirit of God—so that from Jerusalem and all the way around to Illyricum I have fulfilled the ministry of the gospel of Christ; and thus I make it my ambition to preach the gospel, not where Christ has already been named, lest I build on someone else's foundation, but as it is written, "Those who have never been told of him will see, and those who have never heard will understand."

Question 5: What has Christ accomplished through Paul in these verses? How has Christ accomplished this mission through Paul?

---

2. John Piper, "Declare His Glory among the Nations," an online sermon at www.Desiring God.org.

Question 6: What does Paul mean when he says that he has fulfilled the ministry of the gospel of Christ? Does this mean that every person was converted to Christianity between Jerusalem and Illyricum (present-day Albania)?

What in the world did Paul mean that he had no room for work from Jerusalem to Illyricum? It is not a risk to say that there were tens of thousands of people yet to be evangelized in those regions. In other words, there are people that need to be evangelized. And Paul says his work is done in this region.

We take that to mean: Paul is not a local evangelist; he's a frontier missionary, a pioneer missionary. That is, his calling and his ambition is not to do evangelism where the church has been planted. The church should do that. Paul's calling and his ambition is to preach the gospel where there is no evangelizing church. There are no Christians. They don't even know the name.

The terminology is not what's crucial. What's crucial is the distinction. There are frontier or pioneer missionaries, and there are evangelists. Missionaries cross cultures and learn languages. And frontier missionaries pour out their lives "by word and deed, by the power of signs and wonders, by the power of the Spirit of God" to break through thousands of years of darkness and the reign of Satan over a people who do not know the King of kings and the Savior of the world.[3]

Day 4—The Eternality of Hell

One of the things that severs the urgency of missions to unreached peoples is the denial of the doctrine of hell. In our day, some hold that

---

3. John Piper, "Holy Ambition: To Preach Where Christ Has Not Been Named," an online sermon at www.DesiringGod.org.

hell is only temporary and that after a time of purification, all people will be received into glory. Others affirm that unbelievers are simply annihilated. John Piper writes on the importance of the doctrine of eternal conscious punishment and its implications on missions.

Biblical answers to these three questions[4] are crucial because in each case a negative answer would seem to cut a nerve of urgency in the missionary cause. . . .

There is a felt difference in the urgency when one believes that hearing the gospel is the only hope that anyone has of escaping the penalty of sin and living forever in happiness to the glory of God's grace. It does not ring true when William Crockett and James Sigountos argue that the existence of "implicit Christians" (saved through general revelation without hearing Christ) actually "should increase motivation" for missions. They say that these unevangelized converts are "waiting eagerly to hear more about [God]." If we would reach them, "a strong church would spring to life, giving glory to God and evangelizing their pagan neighbors." I cannot escape the impression that this is a futile attempt to make a weakness look like a strength. On the contrary, common sense presses another truth on us: The more likely it is that people can be saved without missions, the less urgency there is for missions.[5]

Study Mark 9:43–48; Matthew 18:8–9; and Matthew 25:46.

Mark 9:43–48

And if your hand causes you to sin, cut it off. It is better for you to enter life crippled than with two hands to go to hell, to the unquenchable fire. And if your foot causes you to sin, cut it off. It is better for you to enter life lame than with two feet to be thrown into hell. And if your eye causes you to sin, tear it out. It is better for you to enter the kingdom of God with one eye

---

4. (1) Will anyone experience *eternal conscious torment* under God's wrath? (2) Is the work of Christ the *necessary* means provided by God for eternal salvation? (3) Is it necessary for people *to hear of Christ* in order to be eternally saved?

5. John Piper, *Let the Nations Be Glad!* 3rd ed. (Grand Rapids: Baker Academic, 2010), 137.

*than with two eyes to be thrown into hell, "where their worm
does not die and the fire is not quenched."*

Matthew 18:8–9
*And if your hand or your foot causes you to sin, cut it off and
throw it away. It is better for you to enter life crippled or lame
than with two hands or two feet to be thrown into the eternal
fire. And if your eye causes you to sin, tear it out and throw it
away. It is better for you to enter life with one eye than with
two eyes to be thrown into the hell of fire.*

Matthew 25:46
*And these will go away into eternal punishment, but the righ-
teous into eternal life.*

Question 7: What are the different ways that these passages portray
hell? What are the indicators that "eternal" means never-
ending?

Look specifically at what Jesus says to Judas in Matthew 26:24.

Matthew 26:24
*The Son of Man goes as it is written of him, but woe to that
man by whom the Son of Man is betrayed! It would have been
better for that man if he had not been born.*

Question 8: Use this text to respond to someone who believes that hell is
a time of purification rather than eternal punishment.

Hell is a dreadful reality. To speak of it lightly proves that we do not grasp its horror. I know of no one who has overstated the terrors of hell. We can scarcely surpass the horrid images Jesus used. We are meant to shudder.

Why? Because the infinite horrors of hell are intended by God to be a vivid demonstration of the infinite value of his glory, which sinners have belittled. The biblical assumption of the justice of hell is the clearest testimony to the infiniteness of the sin of failing to glorify God. All of us have failed. All the nations have failed. Therefore, the weight of infinite guilt rests on every human head because of our failure to delight in God more than we delight in our own self-sufficiency.[6]

Day 5—Through One Man

We saw in the previous day that denying the existence of an eternal conscious place of torment undercuts the urgent nature of missions. Another way that the missionary task is undermined is through denial of the necessity of conscious faith in Jesus in order to be saved. Many people embrace some version of religious pluralism, saying things like, "It doesn't matter in the end who you believe in or follow because all roads eventually lead to the one true God. As long as you genuinely do your best with what you have you will find him in the end."

Question 9: Why do you think this belief is so popular? Write down passages of Scripture that come to mind when you hear claims like the one made above.

---

6. Ibid., 142–43.

There are many Scriptures that testify to the fact that Jesus is the only way to God. We will focus on one of them.

Examine Romans 5:12–21.

Romans 5:12–21

Therefore, just as sin came into the world through one man, and death through sin, and so death spread to all men because all sinned—for sin indeed was in the world before the law was given, but sin is not counted where there is no law. Yet death reigned from Adam to Moses, even over those whose sinning was not like the transgression of Adam, who was a type of the one who was to come.

But the free gift is not like the trespass. For if many died through one man's trespass, much more have the grace of God and the free gift by the grace of that one man Jesus Christ abounded for many. And the free gift is not like the result of that one man's sin. For the judgment following one trespass brought condemnation, but the free gift following many trespasses brought justification. For if, because of one man's trespass, death reigned through that one man, much more will those who receive the abundance of grace and the free gift of righteousness reign in life through the one man Jesus Christ.

Therefore, as one trespass led to condemnation for all men, so one act of righteousness leads to justification and life for all men. For as by the one man's disobedience the many were made sinners, so by the one man's obedience the many will be made righteous. Now the law came in to increase the trespass, but where sin increased, grace abounded all the more, so that, as sin reigned in death, grace also might reign through righteousness leading to eternal life through Jesus Christ our Lord.

Question 10: How does this passage argue for the limitation of salvation to only those who believe and trust in Jesus? Write out the comparisons between Adam and Jesus.

> The crucial point here is *the universality of the work of Christ*. It is not done in a corner with reference merely to Jews. The work of Christ, the second Adam, corresponds to the work of the first Adam. As the sin of Adam leads to condemnation for all humanity that are united to him as their head, so the obedience of Christ leads to righteousness for all humanity that are united to Christ as their head—"those who receive the abundance of grace" (v. 17).[7]
>
> The New Testament makes clear that the atoning work of Christ is not merely for Jews or merely for any one nation or tribe or language. It is the one and only way for anyone to get right with God. The problem of sin is universal, cutting people off from God. The solution to that problem is the atoning death of the Son of God offered once for all. This is the very foundation of missions.[8]

Further Up and Further In

Read "The Echo and Insufficiency of Hell Part 1," an online sermon at www.DesiringGod.org.

Question 11: Where does the path to unorthodoxy usually begin? What other unorthodox beliefs do you perceive having this same beginning?

Many who deny eternal punishment would affirm that "the crime doesn't fit the punishment," meaning that a finite life of rebellion

---

7. Ibid., 145.
8. Ibid., 147.

is not worthy of infinite conscious torment. The belief is that such lengthy punishment undermines the justice and love of God.

Question 12: What are some reasons why annihilationists believe endless suffering is unjust? In what ways is annihilationism unjust? Explain the relationship between God's glory and eternal punishment.

> The righteousness of God is his unswerving commitment to uphold the worth of his glory, and that the desecration of that glory can indeed be "made up" by a just punishment—a corresponding loss of glory. An eternal hell is not unjust, because the sin of a man against an infinitely glorious God is deserving of infinite punishment.[9]

Read the chapter "Missions" in the online book *Desiring God* at www.DesiringGod.org.

Study Romans 1:18–23.

Romans 1:18–23

For the wrath of God is revealed from heaven against all ungodliness and unrighteousness of men, who by their unrighteousness suppress the truth. For what can be known about God is plain to them, because God has shown it to them. For his invisible attributes, namely, his eternal power and divine nature, have been clearly perceived, ever since the creation of the world, in the things that have been made. So they are without excuse. For although they knew God, they did not honor him as God or give thanks to him, but they became futile in their thinking, and their foolish hearts were darkened. Claiming to be wise, they became fools, and exchanged the glory of the immortal God for images resembling mortal man and birds and animals and creeping things.

---

9. John Piper, *The Pleasures of God* (Colorado Springs: Multnomah, 2000), 172.

Question 13: In which way does mankind know God? Would isolated tribes who have never met Christians be included in this group?

The reality of hell for those who have not heard the gospel has been an important motivator for missionaries. However, frontier missions presents an unbelievable set of obstacles and frustrations for the missionary who is interacting with the type of people in Romans 1.
Look at Mark 10:25–27; John 10:16; and Acts 18:9–10.

Mark 10:25–27

"It is easier for a camel to go through the eye of a needle than for a rich person to enter the kingdom of God." And they were exceedingly astonished, and said to him, "Then who can be saved?" Jesus looked at them and said, "With man it is impossible, but not with God. For all things are possible with God."

John 10:16

And I have other sheep that are not of this fold. I must bring them also, and they will listen to my voice. So there will be one flock, one shepherd.

Acts 18:9–10

And the Lord said to Paul one night in a vision, "Do not be afraid, but go on speaking and do not be silent, for I am with you, and no one will attack you to harm you, for I have many in this city who are my people."

Question 14: What do these verses say about the sovereignty of God in salvation?

Question 15: How can these verses be a source of encouragement for the frustrated missionary who sees minimal conversions?

While You Watch the DVD, Take Notes

What are the two astonishing things John Piper says about what Paul writes in Romans 15:15–23?

Summarize the task of missions.

What are the three questions underneath the question "Is missions necessary?"

"The smoke of their _____ goes up _____ and _____ " is the strongest _____ expression for eternity imaginable.

What is the reason for one mediator and not two?

After You Watch the DVD, Discuss What You've Learned

1. Explain the differences in the *method* by which Abraham's commission was to be carried out in Genesis 12 and 17 and the *method* by which the Great Commission is carried out?

2. Discuss the implications for missions if one denies eternal conscious torment. How would you respond to someone who denied or modified the doctrine of hell?

3. Discuss the implications on missions if one believes that Christ's work is not necessary to save people from eternal punishment. How would you respond to someone who believed this?

After You Discuss, Make Application

1. What was the most meaningful part of this lesson for you? Was there a sentence, concept, or idea that really struck you? Why? Record your thoughts in the space below.

2. Write a letter to a friend (real or hypothetical) who denies the doctrine of eternal conscious torment. Seek to briefly persuade them of the importance of this biblical doctrine for missions.

Lesson 4

The Urgency of Missions

Preaching, Hearing, and Believing

Lesson Objectives

It is our prayer that after you have finished this lesson . . .

- You will understand why human beings are accountable to God even when they have not heard of Jesus.
- You will be convinced of the indispensability of the preaching and hearing of the gospel of Christ.
- You will be pressed in greater urgency for unreached peoples.

Before You Watch the DVD, Study and Prepare

Day 1—Will They Be Judged Because They Haven't Heard?

Hell is a daunting reality for those who do not put their trust in Jesus. Sometimes human emotions will get in the way of embracing biblical truth like eternal conscious torment, as we've seen with universalists and annihilationists. It is commonly believed by some that because

43

the gospel has not come to a people group then they are exempt from judgment on the basis of ignorance.

Meditate on Romans 1:18–23.

Romans 1:18–23

For the wrath of God is revealed from heaven against all ungodliness and unrighteousness of men, who by their unrighteousness suppress the truth. For what can be known about God is plain to them, because God has shown it to them. For his invisible attributes, namely, his eternal power and divine nature, have been clearly perceived, ever since the creation of the world, in the things that have been made. So they are without excuse. For although they knew God, they did not honor him as God or give thanks to him, but they became futile in their thinking, and their foolish hearts were darkened. Claiming to be wise, they became fools, and exchanged the glory of the immortal God for images resembling mortal man and birds and animals and creeping things.

Question 1: Are people judged because they have not heard the gospel? What is the reason given in the passage for why the wrath of God is revealed to people?

But if God's divine nature is clearly revealed in his creation, is it possible for some to respond in faith to what God has revealed there, even if they have never heard of Jesus? John Piper addresses this question.

The question that concerns us here is whether some (perhaps only a few) people are quickened by the Holy Spirit and saved by grace through faith in a merciful Creator even though they never hear of Jesus in this life. In other words, are there devout people in other religions who humbly rely on the grace of the God whom they know through nature (Rom. 1:19–21) and thus receive eternal salvation?

> Something of immense historical significance happened with the coming of the Son of God into the world. So great was the significance of this event that the focus of saving faith was henceforth made to center on Jesus Christ alone. So fully does Christ sum up all the revelation of God and all the hopes of God's people that it would henceforth be a dishonor to him should saving faith repose on anyone but him.[1]

Imagine that one of your non-Christian friends heard you explaining that those who do not hear of Jesus Christ are still held accountable before God. They say:

> So you're saying that the only way in which people are saved is through receiving the gospel message? And God condemns even those who have never heard the gospel? If this is true, this seems incredibly unjust.

Question 2: How would you pastorally and patiently respond to this person? What arguments would you use?

Day 2—Cornelius Believes the Gospel

We have seen that there is yet another way in which the urgency of frontier missions is undercut. Some argue that there are certain peoples who genuinely put their faith in God based on his revelation of himself in nature alone, apart from knowledge of Christ. Those who argue this way often appeal to the story of Cornelius in Acts 10–11.

Study Acts 10:1–2 and 10:30–35.

---

1. John Piper, *Let the Nations Be Glad!* 3rd ed. (Grand Rapids: Baker Academic, 2010), 147–48.

Acts 10:1–2

At Caesarea there was a man named Cornelius, a centurion of what was known as the Italian Cohort, a devout man who feared God with all his household, gave alms generously to the people, and prayed continually to God.

Acts 10:30–35

And Cornelius said, "Four days ago, about this hour, I was praying in my house at the ninth hour, and behold, a man stood before me in bright clothing and said, 'Cornelius, your prayer has been heard and your alms have been remembered before God. Send therefore to Joppa and ask for Simon who is called Peter. He is lodging in the house of Simon, a tanner, by the sea.' So I sent for you at once, and you have been kind enough to come. Now therefore we are all here in the presence of God to hear all that you have been commanded by the Lord." So Peter opened his mouth and said: "Truly I understand that God shows no partiality, but in every nation anyone who fears him and does what is right is acceptable to him."

Question 3: Underline phrases in this passage that might lead someone to believe that Cornelius was saved before hearing of Jesus.

Examine Acts 10:43 and 11:13–14.

Acts 10:43

To him all the prophets bear witness that everyone who believes in him receives forgiveness of sins through his name.

Acts 11:13–14

And he told us how he had seen the angel stand in his house and say, "Send to Joppa and bring Simon who is called Peter; he will declare to you a message by which you will be saved, you and all your household."

Question 4: How do these verses shed light on what you saw in Question 3? What conclusions can we draw from the story of Cornelius?

My suggestion is that Cornelius represents a kind of unsaved person among an unreached people group who is seeking God in an extraordinary way. Peter is saying that God *accepts* this search as genuine (hence "acceptable" in verse 35) and works wonders to bring that person the gospel of Jesus Christ the way he did through the visions of both Peter on the housetop and Cornelius in the hour of prayer.[2]

Day 3—A Massive Shift in Redemptive History

The person who believes that people don't necessarily have to hear the gospel to obtain eternal life would naturally point to the saints of the Old Testament (like Abraham and David) who did not yet have the revelation of the gospel and yet were saved. But is this an apt comparison?

Reflect on Ephesians 3:4–10.

Ephesians 3:4–10

When you read this, you can perceive my insight into the mystery of Christ, which was not made known to the sons of men in other generations as it has now been revealed to his holy apostles and prophets by the Spirit. This mystery is that the Gentiles are fellow heirs, members of the same body, and partakers of the promise in Christ Jesus through the gospel. Of this gospel I was made a minister according to the gift of God's grace, which was given me by the working of his power. To me, though I am the

2. Ibid., 160.

very least of all the saints, this grace was given, to preach to the Gentiles the unsearchable riches of Christ, and to bring to light for everyone what is the plan of the mystery hidden for ages in God who created all things, so that through the church the manifold wisdom of God might now be made known to the rulers and authorities in the heavenly places.

Question 5: Underline every place Paul says "mystery." Define the mystery according to this text. What is the means of the fulfillment of the mystery? What is the purpose of the revelation of the mystery?

The mystery referred to in Ephesians also has other names within the New Testament. Luke, in Acts 17:30, refers to the "times of ignorance" with the nations. John Piper writes about Acts 17.

> This text comes from Paul's sermon to the Greeks on the Areopagus in Athens. He had noticed an "altar . . . to the unknown god." In other words, just in case there was another god in the universe whom they did not know about, they had put up an altar, hoping that this "unknowing" act of homage would be acceptable to this deity. So Paul said, "What therefore you worship as unknown, this I proclaim to you" (17:23).[3]

Examine Acts 17:29–30.

Acts 17:29–30

Being then God's offspring, we ought not to think that the divine being is like gold or silver or stone, an image formed by the art and imagination of man. The times of ignorance God overlooked, but now he commands all people everywhere to repent.

---

3. Ibid., 152.

Question 6: What does it mean for God to "overlook the times of ignorance"? With what is Paul contrasting God's overlooking
of the times of ignorance? Given the two passages studied
in this day, what changed when Christ came?

So a massive change has occurred in redemptive
history. Before the coming of Christ, a truth was not fully
revealed—namely, that the nations may enter with equal
standing into the household of God (Eph. 2:19). The time
was not yet "full" for this revelation because Christ had
not been revealed from heaven. The glory and honor of
uniting all the peoples was being reserved for him in his
saving work. It is fitting then that the nations be gathered
in only through the preaching of the message of Christ,
whose cross is the peace that creates the worldwide
church (Eph. 2:11–21).

In other words, there is a profound theological reason
why salvation did not spread to the nations before the
incarnation of the Son of God. The reason is that it would
not have been clear that the nations were gathering for
the glory of Christ. God means for his Son to be the
center of worship as the nations receive the word of
reconciliation. For this reason also . . . the preaching of
Christ is the means appointed by God for the ingathering
of the nations.[4]

Day 4—There Is No Other Name

As we continue to explore the question of whether a person must
consciously hear of Jesus Christ in order to be saved, we turn to
another alternative explanation of the biblical witness. Some Christians agree that the work of Christ is the *means* by which people

---

4. Ibid., 149–50.

are saved, but that a person doesn't necessarily need to *know* about this work in order for it to apply to him. John Piper summarizes this viewpoint.

> Salvation comes only through the *work* of Jesus but not only through faith in Jesus. His work can benefit those who relate to God properly without him, for example, on the basis of general revelation in nature.[5]

Peter testifies to the urgent truth that faith in Jesus is necessary in his proclamation to the rulers and elders in Jerusalem in Acts 4. Study Acts 4:12.

Acts 4:12

And there is salvation in no one else, for there is no other name under heaven given among men by which we must be saved.

Question 7: What do the phrases "under heaven" and "among men" say about Jesus? What is implied in Peter's use of "name"? In other words, why didn't he say "person" or "means"?

> Peter is saying something more than that there is no other *source* of saving power that you can be saved by under some *other* name. The point of saying "There is no other *name*" is that we are saved by calling on the name of the Lord Jesus. Calling on his name is our entrance into fellowship with God. If one is saved by Jesus incognito, one does not speak of being saved *by his name*.[6]

Meditate on Romans 10:13–15.

---

5. Ibid., 163.
6. Ibid., 164.

Romans 10:13–15

*For "everyone who calls on the name of the Lord will be saved."
How then will they call on him in whom they have not believed?
And how are they to believe in him of whom they have never
heard? And how are they to hear without someone preaching?
And how are they to preach unless they are sent? As it is written, "How beautiful are the feet of those who preach the good
news!"*

Question 8: Write down the order of events given in these verses, beginning with the sending of the preacher. What conclusion
must we draw from this passage?

Day 5—The Imperishable Seed

There are two more passages that we will look at in order to reinforce
the necessity of gospel proclamation for salvation.
Look at 1 Peter 1:23–25.

1 Peter 1:23–25

*Since you have been born again, not of perishable seed but of
imperishable, through the living and abiding word of God; for
"All flesh is like grass and all its glory like the flower of grass.
The grass withers, and the flower falls, but the word of the
Lord remains forever." And this word is the good news that
was preached to you.*

Question 9: What is the imperishable seed in verse 23? What does this
imperishable seed accomplish? How do you know from
this verse that the word of God referred to in verse 23 is
not general revelation?

Paul not only taught that the preaching and hearing of the gospel is crucial, but he also thought of his own calling in this manner. Near the end of Acts, Paul recounts the words of Jesus to him in his conversion and commission.

Examine Acts 26:16–18.

Acts 26:16–18

But rise and stand upon your feet, for I have appeared to you for this purpose, to appoint you as a servant and witness to the things in which you have seen me and to those in which I will appear to you, delivering you from your people and from the Gentiles—to whom I am sending you to open their eyes, so that they may turn from darkness to light and from the power of Satan to God, that they may receive forgiveness of sins and a place among those who are sanctified by faith in me.

Question 10: Attempt to summarize Paul's understanding of his own purpose and calling.

Christ commissioned Paul with a word of power that actually opens the eyes of the spiritually blind, not so that they can see they are forgiven but so that they can be forgiven. His message delivers from the power of Satan. The picture of nations without the gospel is that they are blind and in the darkness and in bondage to Satan and without forgiveness of sins and unacceptable to God because they are unsanctified.[7]

---

7. Ibid., 170.

Further Up and Further In

Read "How Shall People Be Saved? Part 1," an online sermon found at www.DesiringGod.org.

John Piper says that Romans 10:13–21 is rooted in the overarching question that Paul is trying to address at the beginning of Romans 9.

Reflect on Romans 9:1–6.

Romans 9:1–6

I am speaking the truth in Christ—I am not lying; my conscience bears me witness in the Holy Spirit—that I have great sorrow and unceasing anguish in my heart. For I could wish that I myself were accursed and cut off from Christ for the sake of my brothers, my kinsmen according to the flesh. They are Israelites, and to them belong the adoption, the glory, the covenants, the giving of the law, the worship, and the promises. To them belong the patriarchs, and from their race, according to the flesh, is the Christ who is God over all, blessed forever. Amen. But it is not as though the word of God has failed. For not all who are descended from Israel belong to Israel.

Question 11: What problem does Paul introduce in Romans 9:1–6?

Paul narrows the problem down to unbelief in the Messiah. He continues to remove any further objections in Romans 10:4–21 by explaining the necessity and sufficiency of the gospel for salvation.

Study Romans 10:9.

Romans 10:9

Because, if you confess with your mouth that Jesus is Lord and believe in your heart that God raised him from the dead, you will be saved.

Question 12: What are the two conditions in this text by which we are saved?

Look at Romans 10:17.

Romans 10:17
So faith comes from hearing, and hearing through the word of Christ.

Question 13: What are the implications of this verse in our fight for faith and our personal pursuit of holiness?

> Out of all the armor God gives us to fight Satan, only one piece is used for killing—the sword. It is called the sword of the Spirit (Eph. 6:17). So when Paul says, "Kill sin by the Spirit," I take that to mean, Depend on the Spirit, especially his sword.
>
> What is the sword of the Spirit? It's the Word of God (Eph. 6:17). Here's where faith comes in. "Faith comes from hearing and hearing by the Word of Christ" (Rom. 10:17). The Word of God cuts through the fog of Satan's lies and shows me where true and lasting happiness is to be found. And so the Word helps me stop trusting in the potential of sin to make me happy. Instead the Word entices me to trust in God's promises.
>
> When faith has the upper hand in my heart I am satisfied with Christ and his promises. . . . When my thirst for joy and meaning and passion are satisfied by the presence and promises of Christ, the power of sin is broken. We do not yield to the offer of sandwich meat when we can smell the steak sizzling on the grill.[8]

8. John Piper, *Future Grace* (Sisters, Ore.: Multnomah, 1995), 334–35.

Read "The Word of Faith We Proclaim, Part 2," an online sermon found at www.DesiringGod.org.

In reference to Romans 10:13—Everyone who calls on the name of the Lord will be saved—John Piper says, "Saved, saved, saved. From what? Saved from guilt, saved from condemnation, saved from the wrath of God, saved from hell, saved from sinning. These are precious riches beyond all price. But they are all negative."

Question 14: What is meant in saying that all of these good gifts are negative?

Reflect on Romans 10:12–13.

Romans 10:12–13
For there is no distinction between Jew and Greek; for the same Lord is Lord of all, bestowing his riches on all who call on him. For "everyone who calls on the name of the Lord will be saved."

Question 15: What are the ultimate riches of God referred to in verse 12? What other verses in the Bible address the riches of God?

While You Watch the DVD, Take Notes

What is the last question that John Piper will be addressing?

Why didn't God tell any of the Old Testament patriarchs or prophets to go out to the nations?

What is a goal that John Piper didn't mention in Session 1 that he prays would happen to you now?

What is the task of missions?

Are people perishing? Yes. There is an _____ _____ _____ of torment. Is Christ's worth necessary to save them? Yes. Christ _____ in order to _____ people from it _____ _____. Do you have to hear about that in order to benefit from it forever? Yes. You must _____ it and _____ it to be _____.

After You Watch the DVD, Discuss What You've Learned

1. How were the saints in the Old Testament saved if they didn't yet know of Jesus? Should their context be thought of differently than those peoples today who haven't heard of Jesus? Support your answer.

2. Discuss why the use of the word "name" in passages like Acts 4:12 is important. How does "the name" relate to the glory of God?

3. Attempt to summarize the contents of this lesson in a few short sentences. Why is it so important to be clear on the questions addressed here?

After You Discuss, Make Application

1. What was the most meaningful part of this lesson for you? Was there a sentence, concept, or idea that really struck you? Why? Record your thoughts in the space below.

2. This lesson has raised the stakes. Not only are unbelievers dying and going to eternal conscious torment, but there are people who do not believe because a witness of Jesus is not among them. Write down a personal prayer as a response to this lesson and the urgency it presents.

Lesson 5

The Goal and the Fuel of Missions

Lesson Objectives

It is our prayer that after you have finished this lesson . . .

- You will understand and be able to articulate the *goal* of missions.
- You will understand and be able to articulate the *fuel* of missions.
- You will be exposed to and rejoice in the radical God-centeredness of God.

Before You Watch the DVD, Study and Prepare

Day 1—A Single Passion and Patrick Johnstone

Most of those who have been used mightily by God among the nations have been motivated by a singular passion. This has not been the case only in our day but throughout history. Over the next few days we will look at a few different people who share this passion for the supremacy of God among the nations.

John Piper writes in his preface to *Let the Nations Be Glad!*

> *Let the Nations Be Glad!* is like a little skiff riding on the wake of the massive undertaking of Patrick Johnstone and Jason Mandryk in publishing *Operation World*. Would

that every Christian used this book to know the nations and pray. I look at this great, church-wakening, mission-advancing book, and I ask, "What kind of mindset unleashes such a book?" Listen.

> All the earth-shaking awesome forces unleashed on the world are released by the Lord Jesus Christ. He reigns today. He is in the control room of the universe. He is the only Ultimate Cause; all the sins of man and machinations of Satan ultimately have to enhance the glory and kingdom of our Saviour. This is true of our world today—in wars, famines, earthquakes, or the evil that apparently has the ascendancy. All God's actions are just and loving. We have become too enemy-conscious and can over-do the spiritual warfare aspect of intercession. We need to be more God-conscious so that we can laugh the laugh of faith knowing that we have power over all the power of the enemy (Luke 10:19). He has already lost control because of Calvary where the lamb was slain. What confidence and rest of heart this gives us as we face a world of turmoil and such spiritual need.[1]

Question 1: Summarize in one or two sentences the driving passion behind undertaking an endeavor like that of Patrick Johnstone in *Operation World*?

Question 2: According to Johnstone, what danger must Christians be aware of as they seek to spread the gospel among the nations? What alternative does he present?

---

1. Patrick Johnstone, as quoted by John Piper, *Let the Nations Be Glad!* 3rd ed. (Grand Rapids: Baker Academic, 2010), 11.

Day 2—A Single Passion and John Stott

John Piper has exulted in the God of Romans 1:5. He has found John Stott's commentary on this verse particularly helpful in regard to the honoring of God's name.

Meditate on Romans 1:5.

Romans 1:5
[Jesus Christ] . . . through whom we have received grace and apostleship to bring about the obedience of faith for the sake of his name among all the nations.

John Stott says concerning this verse:

> The highest of missionary motives is neither obedience to the Great Commission (important as that is), nor love for sinners who are alienated and perishing (strong as that incentive is, especially when we contemplate the wrath of God . . .), but rather zeal—burning and passionate zeal— for the glory of Jesus Christ. . . . Only one imperialism is Christian . . . and that is concern for His Imperial Majesty Jesus Christ, and for the glory of his empire.[2]

Question 3: According to Romans 1:5 what is the highest aim of Paul's office and ministry?

Question 4: Why is it important that all Christians have this motive and passion for God's name in their ministry? What practical implications does this passion have on the life of the church and individuals? Explain the effects on a church or individual if they divert from this single passion.

---

2. John Stott, as quoted by Piper in *Let the Nations Be Glad!* 10.

O for the day when more pastors and scholars and missionaries would not just say that but feel it as the driving force of their lives!

The apostle John applies this Christ-exalting passion to all missionaries when he says, "They have gone out *for the sake of the name*" (3 John 7). . . .

Where do such God-centered, Christ-exalting, missions-driven people come from? We believe they come from God-besotted, Christ-addicted, Bible-breathing homes and churches and schools and ministries. . . .

There is a God-enthralled, Christ-treasuring, all-enduring love that pursues the fullness of God in the soul and in the service of Jesus. It is not absorbed in anthropology or methodology or even theology—it is absorbed in God. It cries out with the psalmist, "Let the peoples praise you, O God; let all the peoples praise you! Let the nations be glad and sing for joy. . . . Sing praises to our King, sing praises! For God is the King of all the earth" (Pss. 67:3–4; 47:6–7).

There is a distinct God-magnifying mind-set. It is relentless in bringing God forward again and again. It is spring-loaded to make much of God in anthropology and methodology and theology. It cannot make peace with God-ignoring, God-neglecting planning or preaching or puttering around.[3]

Day 3—A Single Passion and William Carey

William Carey was an English missionary sent to India in 1793. John Piper describes Carey's vision of God.

Missions is not first and ultimate; God is. And these are not just words. The truth is the lifeblood of missionary inspiration and endurance. William Carey, the father of modern missions . . . expressed the connection:

> When I left England, my hope of India's conversion was very strong; but amongst so many obstacles, it would die, unless upheld by God. Well, I have God, and His Word is true. Though the superstitions of the heathen were a

---

3. Piper, *Let the Nations Be Glad!* 10–11.

> thousand times stronger than they are, and the example
> of the Europeans a thousand times worse; though I were
> deserted by all and persecuted by all, yet my faith, fixed
> on the sure Word, would rise above all obstructions and
> overcome every trial. God's cause will triumph.
>
> Carey and thousands like him have been moved and
> carried by the vision of a great and triumphant God. The
> vision must come first. Savoring it in worship precedes
> spreading it in missions.[4]

Question 5: Describe William Carey's hardships in his ministry. What carried him through those hardships? How does the Word of God overcome trials like Carey's?

Question 6: The last paragraph in the quotation above notes that the vision must come first. Why is it important to savor the vision in worship *before* engaging in missions? What are the repercussions if missions comes before savoring the vision?

Day 4—God's Radical God-Centeredness

The witness of Johnstone, Stott, and Carey all point to one grand and glorious conclusion: that the great motive for world missions is the glory and supremacy of God. Today we will see that this motive is not merely ours, but is also God's. Our passion for the supremacy of God is rooted in God's passion for the supremacy of God. And this passion is the life and vitality of missions.

Meditate upon Isaiah 43:6–7; Isaiah 49:3; Psalm 106:8; 1 Samuel 12:22; Ezekiel 36:22–23; Isaiah 43:25; and Psalm 25:11.

---

4. William Carey, as quoted by Piper in *Let the Nations Be Glad!* 38.

Isaiah 43:6–7
*I will say to the north, Give up, and to the south, Do not with-
hold; bring my sons from afar and my daughters from the end of
the earth, everyone who is called by my name, whom I created
for my glory, whom I formed and made.*

Isaiah 49:3
*And he said to me, "You are my servant, Israel, in whom I will
be glorified."*

Psalm 106:8
*Yet he saved them for his name's sake, that he might make
known his mighty power.*

1 Samuel 12:22
*For the LORD will not forsake his people, for his great name's
sake, because it has pleased the LORD to make you a people for
himself.*

Ezekiel 36:22–23
*Therefore say to the house of Israel, Thus says the Lord GOD: It
is not for your sake, O house of Israel, that I am about to act, but
for the sake of my holy name, which you have profaned among
the nations to which you came. And I will vindicate the holiness
of my great name, which has been profaned among the nations,
and which you have profaned among them. And the nations will
know that I am the LORD, declares the Lord GOD, when through
you I vindicate my holiness before their eyes.*

Isaiah 43:25
*I, I am he who blots out your transgressions for my own sake,
and I will not remember your sins.*

Psalm 25:11
For your name's sake, O LORD, pardon my guilt, for it is great.

Question 7: Underline every reference to the name or glory of God.
Make a list from these Old Testament texts of the different things God does for his own sake.

Examine John 12:27–28; Ephesians 1:4–6; Romans 9:17; 15:7; and 2 Thessalonians 1:9–10.[5]

John 12:27–28
"Now is my soul troubled. And what shall I say? 'Father, save me from this hour'? But for this purpose I have come to this hour. Father, glorify your name." Then a voice came from heaven: "I have glorified it, and I will glorify it again."

Ephesians 1:4–6
Even as he chose us in him before the foundation of the world, that we should be holy and blameless before him. In love he predestined us for adoption as sons through Jesus Christ, according to the purpose of his will, to the praise of his glorious grace, with which he has blessed us in the Beloved.

Romans 9:17
For the Scripture says to Pharaoh, "For this very purpose I have raised you up, that I might show my power in you, and that my name might be proclaimed in all the earth."

Romans 15:7
Therefore welcome one another as Christ has welcomed you, for the glory of God.

2 Thessalonians 1:9–10
They will suffer the punishment of eternal destruction, away from the presence of the Lord and from the glory of his might, when he comes on that day to be glorified in his saints, and to be marveled at among all who have believed, because our testimony to you was believed.

Question 8: Likewise, underline every reference to the name or glory of God. Make a list from these New Testament texts of the different things God does for his own sake.

---

5. For an extended list of verses referring to God's passion for his own name, see Piper, *Let the Nations Be Glad!* 41–46.

Day 5—The Chief End of God

Given the list of verses in the previous day, many people would have a problem with the jealousy that God has for himself. Consider this statement:

> The chief end of God is to glorify God and enjoy Himself forever.[6]

Question 9: Do you find this statement controversial? If so, why? If not, why do you think some people might find it controversial?

Suppose a young teenager went around saying the sorts of things about themselves that God does.

"Everything I do for my little sister, I do it for my own sake."

"I forgave my older brother for hitting me. I forgave him so that I could show my mercy to everyone."

"I mowed the lawn, weeded the garden, and resealed the deck in order to show my own strength."

Question 10: Obviously these sorts of statements come across as silly and juvenile. Yet we find God making statements like this throughout the Bible. What is the fundamental difference between the teenager and God in this regard?

---

6. John Piper, *Desiring God* (Sisters, Ore.: Multnomah, 2003), 31.

> The reason this may sound strange is that we are more
> accustomed to think about our duty than God's design.
> And when we do ask about God's design, we are too
> prone to describe it with ourselves at the center of God's
> affections. We may say, for example, that His design is
> to redeem the world. Or to save sinners. Or to restore
> creation. Or the like.
>
> But God's saving designs are penultimate, not
> ultimate. Redemption, salvation, and restoration are not
> God's ultimate goal. These he performs for the sake
> of something greater: namely, the enjoyment He has in
> glorifying Himself.[7]

Further Up and Further In

Read "Is God for Us or for Himself?" an online sermon at www
.DesiringGod.org.

Question 11: In the beginning of the sermon John Piper gives a hypothetical example of the anger he would have if one of
his children didn't know what he cares about. Why is it
important that we know what God is passionate about?
Why should we care?

Question 12: What are the two reasons that people stumble over God's
God-centeredness?

---

7. Ibid.

Question 13: What solution does John Piper offer for those who stumble in this way?

Question 14: What is the difference between God taking pleasure in his own character and perfections and God taking pleasure in his own name?

Question 15: What overlooked fact about praise did John Piper discover in C. S. Lewis?

While You Watch the DVD, Take Notes

What has become a complicating factor in our own country in regards to frontier missions?

What are the two remaining questions that John Piper has left to address?

The way I have come to put it in the book I wrote is that _____
is not the ultimate goal of the world, history, or _____.
_____ is the ultimate goal. _____ exists because
_____ doesn't.

Why is worship the goal of missions?

Why is worship the fuel of missions?

After You Watch the DVD, Discuss What You've Learned

1. Discuss the quotations by Patrick Johnstone, John Stott, and William Carey. Out of anything they said, what stood out to you?

2. One of John Piper's most notable sentences in his book *Let the Nations Be Glad!* is "Missions exists because worship doesn't."[8] Discuss the meaning of this sentence as well as the proper place of missions in the Christian church and life.

----

8. Piper, *Let the Nations Be Glad!* 63.

3. Discuss the God-centeredness of God. What is your reaction to this truth? What remaining questions do you have about it?

After You Discuss, Make Application

1. What was the most meaningful part of this lesson for you? Was there a sentence, concept, or idea that really struck you? Why? Record your thoughts in the space below.

2. Memorize Ephesians 1:3–6 praying that God would stir up within your heart holy affections and a radical passion for the glory of God.

Ephesians 1:3–6

Blessed be the God and Father of our Lord Jesus Christ, who has blessed us in Christ with every spiritual blessing in the heavenly places, even as he chose us in him before the foundation of the world, that we should be holy and blameless before him. In love he predestined us for adoption as sons through Jesus Christ, according to the purpose of his will, to the praise of his glorious grace, with which he has blessed us in the Beloved.

Lesson 6

Prayer

The Power of Missions

Lesson Objectives

It is our prayer that after you have finished this lesson . . .

- You will understand with your head and your heart the depth of God's love for himself and for us displayed in the Son.
- You will have a good grasp of the function of prayer in the Christian life.
- You will see the vital importance of prayer in world evangelization.

Before You Watch the DVD, Study and Prepare

Day 1—The Cost

The last lesson showed from the Bible that God is passionate not only about himself and his own infinite value, but he also is passionate about his value going public. The Old Testament demonstrates clearly that Israel was to be a people who displayed the name and reputation of God so that other nations would be drawn to worship him.

71

However, we also saw that many people have a problem with God's zeal for himself, diagnosing God with a serious case of egomania. Study Ephesians 1:5–6 and Romans 3:25.

Ephesians 1:5–6

[In love] he predestined us for adoption as sons through Jesus Christ, according to the purpose of his will, to the praise of his glorious grace, with which he has blessed us in the Beloved. In him we have redemption through his blood, the forgiveness of our trespasses, according to the riches of his grace.

Romans 3:25

[Christ Jesus] . . . whom God put forward as a propitiation by his blood, to be received by faith. This was to show God's righteousness, because in his divine forbearance he had passed over former sins.

Question 1: How do you know from these verses that God takes the vindication of his name seriously in forgiving sins? What was the cost of God demonstrating his righteousness?

Christ was on a mission to magnify God. He came to show that *God* is truthful. He came to show that *God* is a promise-keeper: And he came to show that *God* is glorious. Jesus came into the world for *God's* sake—to certify *God's* integrity, to vindicate *God's* Word, to magnify *God's* glory. Since God sent his Son to do all this, it is plain that the primary motive of the first great mission to unreached peoples—the mission of Jesus from heaven—was God's zeal for the glory of God.[1]

---

1. John Piper, *Let the Nations Be Glad!* 3rd ed. (Grand Rapids: Baker Academic, 2010), 52.

Question 2: Explain how Christ shows the following:

> that God is truthful
> that God is a promise-keeper
> that God is glorious
> God's integrity
> the vindication of God's word

Day 2—God's Glory Is God's Love

God is not an egomaniac. God is love. "Beloved, let us love one another, for love is from God, and whoever loves has been born of God and knows God. Anyone who does not love does not know God, because God is love" (1 John 4:7–8). But the question still remains: how is God loving in his pursuit of his own glory?

Read 1 Peter 3:18.

1 Peter 3:18
For Christ also suffered once for sins, the righteous for the un-righteous, that he might bring us to God, being put to death in the flesh but made alive in the spirit.

Question 3: We previously saw that God's goal in sending his Son was to display the riches of his mercy. According to this verse what is the goal of Christ's suffering and death? Explain how these two purposes of God can be one and the same.

Do people go to the Grand Canyon to increase their self-esteem? Probably not. This is, at least, a hint that the deepest joys in life come not from savoring the self, but from seeing splendor. We were made to enjoy God.

Both the Old and New Testament tell us that God's loving us is a means to our glorifying him. God's love is the ground. His glory is the goal. This is shocking. The love of God is not God's making much of us, but God's saving us from self-centeredness so that we can enjoy making much of him forever. And our love to others is not our making much of them, but helping them to find satisfaction in making much of God. True love aims at satisfying people in the glory of God. Any love that terminates on man is eventually destructive. It does not lead people to the only lasting joy, namely, God. Love must be God-centered, or it is not true love; it leaves people without their final hope of joy.

It is profoundly wrong to turn the cross into a proof that self-esteem is the root of mental health. If I stand before the love of God and do not feel a healthy, satisfying, freeing joy unless I turn that love into an echo of my self-esteem, then I am like a man who stands before the Grand Canyon and feels no satisfying wonder until he translates the canyon into a case for his own significance. That is not the presence of mental health, but bondage to self.[2]

Question 4: Attempt to use an everyday example, like the Grand Canyon, to write out a brief explanation of why God's invitation to glorify himself is in fact an expression of his love.

---

2. John Piper, "The Goal of God's Love May Not Be What You Think It Is," an online sermon at www.DesiringGod.org.

Day 3—What Is Love?

Look at the account of Lazarus in John 11:1–6.

John 11:1–6
Now a certain man was ill, Lazarus of Bethany, the village of Mary and her sister Martha. It was Mary who anointed the Lord with ointment and wiped his feet with her hair, whose brother Lazarus was ill. So the sisters sent to him, saying, "Lord, he whom you love is ill." But when Jesus heard it he said, "This illness does not lead to death. It is for the glory of God, so that the Son of God may be glorified through it." Now Jesus loved Martha and her sister and Lazarus. So, when he heard that Lazarus was ill, he stayed two days longer in the place where he was.

Question 5: Explain the presence of the word "so" in verse 6. What did Jesus do on account of his love for Martha, her sister, and Lazarus?

Question 6: Connect the love of God for Mary, Martha, and Lazarus to Jesus' commitment to the glory of God.

Day 4—The Question of "How?"

The fuel of missions is worship. The goal of missions is worship. Our worship is a commitment to the glory of God's name just as God's worship is his own commitment to the glory of his name. So how do we do missions in light of this magnificent truth?

Question 7: What tools has God given to the church in order to accomplish the mission of magnifying his name among the nations?

Examine Romans 1:16; 10:17; James 1:18; 1 Peter 1:23; and Acts 19:20.

Romans 1:16
For I am not ashamed of the gospel, for it is the power of God for salvation to everyone who believes, to the Jew first and also to the Greek.

Romans 10:17
So faith comes from hearing, and hearing through the word of Christ.

James 1:18
Of his own will he brought us forth by the word of truth, that we should be a kind of firstfruits of his creatures.

1 Peter 1:23
Since you have been born again, not of perishable seed but of imperishable, through the living and abiding word of God.

Acts 19:20
So the word of the Lord continued to increase and prevail mightily.

Question 8: What does the word of God accomplish in each of these passages? Underline key phrases.

Here we must be careful. The role of prayer is so unspeakably significant in God's design that we are prone to overstate its role, especially in relation to the Word of God and the preaching of the Gospel. So let me say, loud and clear, that I believe the proclamation of the Gospel in word and deed is the work of missions. And prayer is the power that wields the weapon of the Word, and the Word is the weapon by which the nations will be brought to faith and obedience.[3]

Day 5—Wartime Walkie-Talkie

Life is war. That's not all it is. But it is always that. Our weakness in prayer is owing largely to our neglect of this truth. Prayer is primarily a wartime walkie-talkie for the mission of the church as it advances against the powers of darkness and unbelief. It is not surprising that prayer malfunctions when we try to make it a domestic intercom to call upstairs for more comforts in the den. God has given us prayer as a wartime walkie-talkie so that we can call headquarters for everything we need as the kingdom of Christ advances in the world. Prayer gives us the significance of frontline forces and gives God the glory of a limitless Provider. The one who gives the power gets the glory. Thus, prayer safeguards the supremacy of God in missions while lining us with endless grace for every need.[4]

Question 9: If you were to ask a person on the street what prayer is for, what do you think he would say? Would the answer be different if he was a Christian as opposed to an unbeliever?

3. John Piper, "Prayer: The Work of Missions," an online sermon at www.DesiringGod .org.
4. Piper, *Let the Nations Be Glad!* 65.

Until you believe that life is war, you cannot know what
prayer is for. Prayer is for the accomplishment of a
wartime mission. It is as though the field commander
(Jesus) called in the troops, gave them a crucial mission
("Go and bear fruit"), handed each of them a personal
transmitter coded to the frequency of the general's
headquarters, and said, "Comrades, the general has a
mission for you. He aims to see it accomplished. And
to that end he has authorized me to give each of you
personal access to him through these transmitters. If
you stay true to his mission and seek his victory first,
he will always be as close as your transmitter, to give
tactical advice and to send in air cover when you or your
comrades need it."

But what have millions of Christians done? They have
stopped believing that we are in a war. No urgency, no
watching, no vigilance, no strategic planning. Just easy
peacetime and prosperity. And what did they do with the
walkie-talkie? They tried to rig it up as an intercom in their
cushy houses and cabins and boats and cars—not to call
in firepower for conflict with a mortal enemy, but to ask
the maid to bring another pillow to the den.[5]

Question 10: What flawed view of prayer does John Piper address in
this passage? What gives rise to this flawed view of prayer?
Give any examples of this flawed approach to prayer that
you've encountered.

Further Up and Further In

Read "Prayer: The Power of Christian Hedonism," a chapter in the
online book *Desiring God* at www.DesiringGod.org.

---

5. Piper, "Prayer," an online sermon at www.DesiringGod.org.

Question 11: In the beginning of this chapter John Piper states that prayer "is the pursuit of God's glory" and prayer "is the pursuit of our joy." In two sentences explain how prayer is each one of these.

One of the effects of prayer is that it creates a dependency which produces humility.

Question 12: Given that many people spend much of their lives seeking to make a name for themselves, how is it possible that prayerful dependence can increase our joy?

Humility is important because it is God's pathway to infinite pleasure. Better humble and poor than proud and rich. Really? Why? 1 Peter 5:5, "Clothe yourselves all of you with humility toward one another, for God opposes the proud, but gives grace to the humble." Poor humility is better than rich pride, because God is against the proud. Even his riches will be a snare to bring him to ruin in the end. If God is opposed to you, to whom can you turn for help? But he gives grace to the humble. He is watching like a jealous lioness over all his lowly cubs. And not only is he watching; he is close to the lowly and refreshes them when they are about to fall. He loves to magnify the height of his grace by condescending to the lowly. Isaiah 57:15, "For thus says the high and lofty One who inhabits eternity, 'I dwell in the high and holy place and also with him who is of a contrite and humble spirit, to revive the spirit of the humble and to revive the heart of the contrite.'" What a promise! You cannot be too insignificant for God to reach you; he loves to dwell with the lowly and contrite. That is bad news for the proud and self-reliant, but good news for broken sinners.[6]

Question 13: When does prayer become idolatrous? Does prayer become idolatrous if the chief end is your own happiness? Explain your answer.

Question 14: What startling warning does John Piper give in this chapter?

Examine Acts 17:24–25.

Acts 17:24–25

The God who made the world and everything in it, being Lord of heaven and earth, does not live in temples made by man, nor is he served by human hands, as though he needed anything, since he himself gives to all mankind life and breath and everything.

Question 15: Using this passage, distinguish between service that honors God and service that dishonors him.

6. John Piper, "It's My Pleasure: Humility and Christian Hedonism," an online sermon at www.DesiringGod.org.

While You Watch the DVD, Take Notes

What is the main motive for finishing the Great Commission?

The cross was _____ costly in order to magnify the
_____ of _____ to _____ like
us. He wants us to see it and make _____ of the
_____, not ourselves.

What is the brief reason that John Piper gives as to why God's pursuit
of his own glory is love?

What was the first sentence of John Piper's ACMC sermon, "Prayer:
The Work of Missions"?

You cannot know what _____ is for until you know that
_____ is _____.

After You Watch the DVD, Discuss What You've Learned

1. Continue to reflect on the relationship between the love of God
   and the glory of God. What new insights did you see in this lesson? What questions still remain in your mind?

2. Discuss the account of Mary and Lazarus in John 11:1–6. Why is the word "so" or "therefore" important in describing the love of God? What does this tell you about God's glory in relation to our happiness?

3. Discuss the view of prayer presented in this lesson. How does it differ from the way that you've viewed prayer in the past? How does it differ from other perspectives on prayer that you've encountered?

After You Discuss, Make Application

1. What was the most meaningful part of this lesson for you? Was there a sentence, concept, or idea that really struck you? Why? Record your thoughts in the space below.

2. Make a list of ten wartime prayer points that relate specifically to the advance of the gospel to unreached peoples. This could be for one particular people or ten different peoples. The points could be for a specific missionary or a group of missionaries. After you have developed these ten points, spend significant time asking the Lord to meet these needs.

Lesson 7

Suffering

The Cost of Missions

Lesson Objectives

It is our prayer that after you have finished this lesson . . .

- You will see the purpose of prayer.
- You will understand that suffering is necessary in the Christian life.
- You will capture a vision of suffering for the glory of God among the nations.

Before You Watch the DVD, Study and Prepare

Day 1—Ask the Father

In this session we will continue our study on prayer, its function in the life of the Christian, and its relationship to world missions and the advance of the gospel.

Examine Ephesians 6:17–18.

Ephesians 6:17–18
And take the helmet of salvation, and the sword of the Spirit,
which is the word of God, praying at all times in the Spirit,
with all prayer and supplication. To that end keep alert with
all perseverance, making supplication for all the saints.

Question 1: Underline the portion of this verse that addresses prayer.
How does verse 17 relate to verse 18? Given this relationship explain how prayer is functioning in these verses.

Study John 15:16.

John 15:16
You did not choose me, but I chose you and appointed you that
you should go and bear fruit and that your fruit should abide,
so that whatever you ask the Father in my name, he may give
it to you.

Question 2: Underline the portion of this verse that addresses prayer.
What is the purpose of the saints' fruit-bearing? In light
of this, what is the purpose of prayer?

The logic is crucial. Why is the Father going to give the
disciples what they ask in Jesus' name? Answer: Because
they have been sent to bear fruit. The reason the Father
gives the disciples the gift of prayer is because Jesus has
given them a mission. In fact, the grammar of John 15:16
implies that the reason Jesus gives them their mission
is so that they will be able to enjoy the power of prayer. "I
send you to bear fruit so that whatever you ask the Father

> . . . he may give you." So I do not tire of saying to our church, The number one reason why prayer malfunctions in the hands of believers is that they try to turn a wartime walkie-talkie into a domestic intercom.[1]

Day 2—The Sovereignty of God and Prayer

Reflect on the Lord's Prayer in Matthew 6:9–13.

Matthew 6:9–13
Pray then like this: "Our Father in heaven, hallowed be your name. Your kingdom come, your will be done, on earth as it is in heaven. Give us this day our daily bread, and forgive us our debts, as we also have forgiven our debtors. And lead us not into temptation, but deliver us from evil."

Question 3: Make a list of every request in Jesus' prayer. Write down any observations you have as to the nature of each request.

One question that often arises in discussions about prayer is how it relates to the sovereignty of God.

---

1. John Piper, "Prayer: The Work of Missions," an online sermon at www.DesiringGod.org.

Question 4: How would you answer the following question: "If you believe God has ordained all things and that his knowledge of all things is exhaustive and infallible, then what is the point of praying that anything happen?"

Prayer is like preaching in that it is a human act also. It is a human act that God has ordained and which he delights in because it reflects the dependence of his creatures upon Him. He has promised to respond to prayer, and his response is just as contingent upon our prayer as our prayer is in accordance with his will.

In other words, just as God will see to it that His Word is proclaimed as a means to saving the elect, so He will see to it that all those prayers are prayed which He has promised to respond to. I think Paul's words in Romans 15:18 would apply equally well to his preaching and his praying ministry: "I will not presume to speak of anything except what Christ has accomplished through me, resulting in the obedience of the Gentiles." Even our prayers are a gift from the one who "works in us that which is pleasing in his sight" (Heb. 13:21). Oh, how grateful we should be that He has chosen us to be employed in this high service! How eager we should be to spend much time in prayer![2]

Day 3—We Will Suffer

We have seen that prayer is the power behind our missionary endeavors. We turn now to examine the role of suffering in the spread of the gospel.

---

2. John Piper, "The Sovereignty of God and Prayer," an online article at www.DesiringGod .org.

Question 5: As we begin this section, make a list of reasons why God might send suffering into the lives of his people.

Look at John 15:20 and Acts 14:21–22.

John 15:20
Remember the word that I said to you: "A servant is not greater than his master." If they persecuted me, they will also persecute you. If they kept my word, they will also keep yours.

Acts 14:21–22
When they had preached the gospel to that city and had made many disciples, they returned to Lystra and to Iconium and to Antioch, strengthening the souls of the disciples, encouraging them to continue in the faith, and saying that through many tribulations we must enter the kingdom of God.

Question 6: What are the reasons given from this text as to why those who are in Christ are to suffer?

Some suffering is the calling of every believer but especially of those God calls to bear the gospel to the unreached. Dietrich Bonhoeffer's famous lines are biblical: "The cross is not the terrible end to an otherwise God-fearing and happy life, but it meets us at the beginning of our communion with Christ. When Christ calls a man, he bids him come and die." This is simply a paraphrase of Mark 8:34: "If anyone would come after me, let him deny himself and *take up his cross* and follow me." To take up a cross and follow Jesus means to join Jesus on the Calvary road with a resolve to suffer and die with him. The cross is not a burden to bear; it is an instrument of pain and execution. It would be like saying, "Pick up your electric chair and follow me to the execution room." Or "Pick up this sword and carry it to the place of beheading." Or "Take up this rope and carry it to the gallows."[3]

Day 4—The Purposes in the Sufferings of the Saints

Read 1 Peter 4:12–13.

1 Peter 4:12–13
Beloved, do not be surprised at the fiery trial when it comes upon you to test you, as though something strange were happening to you. But rejoice insofar as you share Christ's sufferings, that you may also rejoice and be glad when his glory is revealed.

Question 7: What are Peter's two commands in this passage? What is the purpose of the command in verse 13? How does joy in suffering work toward joy and gladness at the coming of Jesus?

Study 2 Timothy 3:12; 2 Corinthians 1:8; and 2 Corinthians 12:9.

2 Timothy 3:12
Indeed, all who desire to live a godly life in Christ Jesus will be persecuted.

2 Corinthians 1:8
For we do not want you to be ignorant, brothers, of the affliction we experienced in Asia. For we were so utterly burdened beyond our strength that we despaired of life itself. Indeed, we felt that

---

3. John Piper, *Let the Nations Be Glad!* 3rd ed. (Grand Rapids: Baker Academic, 2010), 96.

*we had received the sentence of death. But that was to make us
rely not on ourselves but on God who raises the dead.*

2 Corinthians 12:9

*But he said to me, "My grace is sufficient for you, for my power
is made perfect in weakness." Therefore I will boast all the more
gladly of my weaknesses, so that the power of Christ may rest
upon me.*

Question 8: Each of these passages describes a different purpose in
the sufferings of the Christian. Identify these purposes
and explain how suffering works toward them.

The domestication of cross-bearing into coughs and
cranky spouses takes the radical thrust out of Christ's
call. He is calling every believer to "renounce all that
he has," to "hate his own life" (Luke 14:33, 26), and to
take the road of obedience joyfully, no matter the loss
on this earth. Following Jesus means that wherever
obedience requires it, we will accept betrayal and
rejection and beating and mockery and crucifixion and
death. Jesus gives us the assurance that if we will follow
him to Golgotha during all the Good Fridays of this life,
we will also rise with him on the last Easter day of the
resurrection. "Whoever loses his life for my sake and the
gospel's will save it" (Mark 8:35). "Whoever hates his life
in this world will keep it for eternal life" (John 12:25).[4]

Day 5—Where Love Is Pursued, Life Is Taken

The cost of following Jesus will be our lives. But the Lord promises
wonderful things for the suffering saint. We have seen that joy and

---

4. Ibid.

gladness, future glory, and increased faith are all results of the pain
the God brings into our lives. But how does all of this teaching on
suffering apply to what we've been studying, namely missions?
Meditate on Matthew 5:11–16.

Matthew 5:11–16

*Blessed are you when others revile you and persecute you and
utter all kinds of evil against you falsely on my account. Rejoice
and be glad, for your reward is great in heaven, for so they persecuted the prophets who were before you. You are the salt of
the earth, but if salt has lost its taste, how shall its saltiness be
restored? It is no longer good for anything except to be thrown
out and trampled under people's feet. You are the light of the
world. A city set on a hill cannot be hidden. Nor do people light
a lamp and put it under a basket, but on a stand, and it gives
light to all in the house. In the same way, let your light shine
before others, so that they may see your good works and give
glory to your Father who is in heaven.*

Question 9: Break this passage into three divisions of thought. What
is the logical connection between these divisions? How
does this passage relate to unreached peoples?

More and more I am persuaded from Scripture and
from the history of missions that God's design for the
evangelization of the world and the consummation of
his purposes includes the suffering of his ministers and
missionaries. To put it more plainly and specifically, God
designs that the suffering of his ambassadors is one
essential means in the triumphant spread of the Good
News among all the peoples of the world. I am saying
more than the obvious fact that suffering is a result of
faithful obedience in spreading the gospel. That is true. I
am saying that this suffering is part of God's strategy for

> making known to the world who Christ is, how he loves, and how much he is worth.
>
> Suffering and death in the place of sinners was the way that Christ accomplished salvation. "Christ redeemed us from the curse of the law by becoming a curse for us" (Gal. 3:13). "He was wounded for our transgressions; he was crushed for our iniquities" (Isa. 53:5). We preach that. It is the heart of the gospel. But this voluntary suffering and death to save others is not only the content but it is also the method of our mission. We proclaim the Good News of what he accomplished, and we join him in the Calvary method. We embrace his sufferings for us, and we spread the gospel by our suffering with him.[5]

Question 10: Interact with the quotation above. What is your reaction to this passage? What questions does it raise in your mind?

Further Up and Further In

Read "Doing Missions When Dying Is Gain," an online sermon at www.DesiringGod.org.

John Piper cites Steve Saint's testimony.

> Steve Saint tells the story of his dad getting speared by Auca Indians in Ecuador. He tells it after having learned new details of intrigue in the Auca tribe that were responsible for this killing when it shouldn't have happened, and seemingly wouldn't have and couldn't have. Yet it did happen. And having discovered the intrigue he wrote this article. He said,
>
> "As [the natives] described their recollections, it occurred to me how incredibly unlikely it was that the

---

5. John Piper, *Filling Up the Afflictions of Christ* (Wheaton: Crossway Books, 2009), 14–15.

palm beach killing took place at all. It is an anomaly that I
cannot explain outside of divine intervention."

Question 11: What is the anomaly according to Steve Saint? What do
you think Steve means by the final sentence?

Read Colossians 1:24.

Colossians 1:24
*Now I rejoice in my sufferings for your sake, and in my flesh I
am filling up what is lacking in Christ's afflictions for the sake
of his body, that is, the church.*

Question 12: What does it mean to "rejoice in sufferings"? Is this nothing more than masochistic tendencies?

Question 13: Read the wider context of Colossians 1:24. What does
Paul mean when he says that he is "filling up what is
lacking in Christ's afflictions"?

In his sufferings Paul is "filling up what is lacking in Christ's afflictions for . . . the church." What does that mean? It means that Paul's sufferings fill up Christ's afflictions not by adding anything to their worth, but by extending them to the people they were meant to save.

What is lacking in the afflictions of Christ is not that they are deficient in worth, as though they could not sufficiently cover the sins of all who believe. What is lacking is that the infinite value of Christ's afflictions is not known and trusted in the world. These afflictions and what they mean are still hidden to most peoples. And God's intention is that the mystery be revealed to all the nations. So the afflictions of Christ are "lacking" in the sense that they are not seen and known and loved among the nations. They must be carried by missionaries. And those missionaries "complete" what is lacking in the afflictions of Christ by extending them to others.[6]

Reflect on Hebrews 10:32–34.

Hebrews 10:32–34

But recall the former days when, after you were enlightened, you endured a hard struggle with sufferings, sometimes being publicly exposed to reproach and affliction, and sometimes being partners with those so treated. For you had compassion on those in prison, and you joyfully accepted the plundering of your property, since you knew that you yourselves had a better possession and an abiding one.

Question 14: How does the author of the book of Hebrews encourage these saints to persevere? To what does he draw their attention?

---

6. Ibid., 22.

Meditate on Romans 8:35–39.

Romans 8:35–39

Who shall separate us from the love of Christ? Shall tribulation, or distress, or persecution, or famine, or nakedness, or danger, or sword? As it is written, "For your sake we are being killed all the day long; we are regarded as sheep to be slaughtered." No, in all these things we are more than conquerors through him who loved us. For I am sure that neither death nor life, nor angels nor rulers, nor things present nor things to come, nor powers, nor height nor depth, nor anything else in all creation, will be able to separate us from the love of God in Christ Jesus our Lord.

Question 15: Underline anything in this passage that has to do with suffering. How does this passage uphold the Christian who is suffering? Explain how Paul's exhortation could embolden certain individuals for radical ministry to unreached peoples.

While You Watch the DVD, Take Notes

The _____ church has taken a wartime _____ and turned it into a _____ _____.

What illustration does John Piper use to explain the Calvinist's understanding of prayer?

(Fill in the blanks using the choices below.)

There is no vacation from the devil. There is no vacation from war. There is only relief at the end. The devil _____ us, and he is _____ us.

(a) neglects / indifferent to
(b) hates / more powerful than
(c) hates / weaker than
(d) is apathetic to / just as powerful as

In reference to Matthew 5:13, what makes the good deeds "tasty"?

What is the foundation of the work of missions? What is the motive of missions? What is the cost of missions?

After You Watch the DVD, Discuss What You've Learned

1. What is the connection between the sovereignty of God and prayer? Interact with the common objection people have with prayer and God's sovereignty. How does believing in God's sovereignty with prayer empower the missions movement?

2. How has this lesson changed your perspective on hardships and suffering?

3. Record any remaining questions you have about the subjects covered in this lesson. Time permitting, bring them up in your group.

After You Discuss, Make Application

1. What was the most meaningful part of this lesson for you? Was there a sentence, concept, or idea that really struck you? Why? Record your thoughts in the space below.

2. John Piper often describes three categories that every Christian falls under in regards to missions. "You can be a goer, you can be a sender, or you can be disobedient." We're praying at this point you would fall under the first two. Write down ways in which you can choose a path of suffering as a goer or a sender. This can be anything from choosing to sacrifice comforts of time and money to support your local missionaries to being the local missionary who is supported. When you are done, ask the Lord to move your heart to pursue one or many of these avenues.

Lesson 8

Review and Conclusion

Lesson Objectives

. . . .

It is our prayer that after you have finished this lesson . . .

- You will be able to summarize and synthesize what you've learned.
- You will hear what others in your group have learned.
- You will share with others how you have begun to see suffering in a new light.

. . . .

What Have You Learned?

There are no study questions to answer in preparation for this lesson. Instead, spend your time writing a few paragraphs that explain what you've learned in this group study. To help you do this, you may choose to review the notes you've taken in the previous lessons. Then, after you've written down what you've learned, write down some questions that still remain in your mind about anything addressed in these lessons.

Be prepared to share these reflections and questions with the group in the next lesson.

Notes

Use this space to record anything in the group discussion that you want to remember:

Leader's Guide

As the leader of this group study, **it is imperative that you are completely familiar with this study guide** and with the *Let the Nations Be Glad!* DVD Set. Therefore, it is our strong recommendation that you (1) read and understand the introduction, (2) skim each lesson, surveying its layout and content, and (3) read the entire Leader's Guide *before* you begin the group study and distribute the study guides. As you review this Leader's Guide, keep in mind that the material here is only a recommendation. As the leader of the study, feel free to adapt this study guide to your situation and context.

Before Lesson 1

Before the first lesson, you will need to know approximately how many participants you will have in your group study. **Each participant will need their own study guide!** Therefore, be sure to order enough study guides. You will distribute these study guides at the beginning of the first lesson.

It is also our strong recommendation that you, as the leader, familiarize yourself with this study guide and the *Let the Nations Be Glad!* DVD Set in order to answer any questions that might arise and also to ensure that each group session runs smoothly and maximizes the learning of the participants. It is not necessary for you to preview *Let the Nations Be Glad!* in its entirety—although it certainly wouldn't hurt!—but you should be prepared to navigate your way through each DVD menu.

NOTE: As we stated in the Introduction, this study guide is designed for an eight-session guided study. However, we understand that there are times when a group may only have six weeks with which to complete this study. In such a case, we recommend abbreviating Lesson 1 and completing it along with Lesson 2 in the first week. The preparatory work for Lesson 2 can be completed as a group during the first session. In addition, Lesson 8 may be completed by the student on their own after the group has met for the final time.

During Lesson 1

Each lesson is designed for a one-hour group session. Lessons 2–8 require preparatory work from the participant before this group session. Lesson 1, however, requires no preparation on the part of the participant.

The following format is suggested for the first hour of your group study.

Introduction to the Study Guide (10 minutes)

Introduce this study guide and the *Let the Nations Be Glad!* DVD. Share with the group why you chose to lead the group study using these resources. Inform your group of the commitment that this study will require and motivate them to work hard. Pray for the eight-week study, asking God for the grace you will need. Then distribute one study guide to each participant. You may read the introduction aloud, if you want, or you may immediately turn the group to Lesson 1 (starting on page 11 of this study guide).

Personal Introductions (15 minutes)

Since group discussion will be an integral part of this guided study, it is crucial that each participant feels welcome and safe. The goal of each lesson is for every participant to contribute to the discussion in some way. Therefore, during these 15 minutes, have the participants introduce themselves. You may choose to use the questions listed in the section entitled "About Yourself," or you may ask questions of your own choosing.

Discussion (25 minutes)

Transition from the time of introductions to the discussion questions listed under the heading "A Preview of *Let the Nations Be Glad!*" Invite everyone in the class to respond to these questions, but don't let the discussion become too involved. These questions are designed to spark interest and generate questions. The aim is not to come to definitive answers yet.

Review and Closing (10 minutes)

End the group session by reviewing Lesson 2 with the group participants and informing them of the preparation that they must do before the group meets again. Encourage them to be faithful in preparing for the next lesson. Answer any questions that the group may have and then close in prayer.

Before Lessons 2–7

As the group leader, you should do all the preparation for each lesson that is required of the group participants, that is, the ten study questions. Furthermore, it is highly recommended that you complete the entire "Further Up and Further In" section. This is not required of the group participants, but it will enrich your preparation and help you to guide and shape the conversation more effectively.

The group leader should also preview the session of *Let the Nations Be Glad!* that will be covered in the next lesson. So, for example, if the group participants are doing the preparatory work for Lesson 3, you should preview *Let the Nations Be Glad!* Session 2, before the group meets and views it. Previewing each session will better equip you to understand the material and answer questions. If you want to pause the DVD in the midst of the session in order to clarify or discuss, previewing the session will allow you to plan where you want to take your pauses.

Finally, you may want to supplement or modify the discussion questions or the application assignment. Please remember that **this study guide is a resource**; any additions or changes you make that better match the study to your particular group are encouraged. As the group leader, your own discernment, creativity, and guidance are invaluable, and you should adapt the material as you see fit.

Plan for about two hours of your own preparation before each lesson!

During Lessons 2–7

Again, let us stress that during Lessons 2–7, you may use the group time in whatever way you desire. The following format, however, is what we suggest.

Discussion (10 minutes)

Begin your time with prayer. The tone you set in your prayer will likely be impressed upon the group participants: if your prayer is serious and heartfelt, the group participants will be serious about prayer; if your prayer is hasty, sloppy, or a token gesture, the group participants will share this same attitude toward prayer. So model the kind of praying that you desire your students to imitate. Remember, the blood of Jesus has bought your access to the throne of grace.

After praying, review the preparatory work that the participants completed. How did they answer the questions? Which questions did they find to be the most interesting or the most confusing? What observations or insights can they share with the group? If you would like to review some tips for leading productive discussion, please turn to the appendix at the end of this Leader's Guide.

The group participants will be provided an opportunity to apply what they've learned in Lessons 2–7. As the group leader, you can choose whether it would be appropriate for the group to discuss these assignments during this ten-minute time-slot.

DVD Viewing (30 minutes)[1]

Play the session of *Let the Nations Be Glad!* that corresponds to the lesson you're studying. You may choose to pause the DVD at crucial

---

1. Thirty minutes is only an approximation. Some of the sessions are shorter while some are longer. You may need to budget your group time differently, depending upon which session you are viewing.

points to check for understanding and provide clarification. Or, you may choose to watch the DVD without interruption.

Discussion and Closing (20 minutes)

Foster discussion on what was taught during John Piper's session. You may do this by first reviewing the DVD notes (under the heading "While You Watch the DVD, Take Notes") and then proceeding to the discussion questions, listed under the heading "After You Watch the DVD, Discuss What You've Learned." These discussion questions are meant to be springboards that launch the group into further and deeper discussion. Don't feel constrained to these questions if the group discussion begins to move in other helpful directions.

Close the time by briefly reviewing the application section and the homework that is expected for the next lesson. Pray and dismiss.

Before Lesson 8

It is important that you encourage the group participants to complete the preparatory work for Lesson 8. This assignment invites the participants to reflect on what they've learned and what remaining questions they still have. As the group leader, this would be a helpful assignment for you to complete as well. In addition, you may want to write down the key concepts of this DVD series that you want the group participants to walk away with.

During Lesson 8

The group participants are expected to complete a reflection exercise as part of their preparation for Lesson 8. The bulk of the group time during this last lesson should be focused on reviewing and synthesizing what was learned. Encourage each participant to share some of their recorded thoughts. Attempt to answer any remaining questions that they might have.

To close this last lesson, you might want to spend extended time in prayer. If appropriate, take prayer requests relating to what the participants have learned in these eight weeks, and bring these requests to God.

It would be completely appropriate for you, the group leader, to give a final charge or word of exhortation to end this group study. Speak from your heart and out of the overflow of joy that you have in God.

Please receive our blessing for all group leaders who choose to use this study guide:

> *The LORD bless you and keep you; the LORD make his face to shine upon you and be gracious to you; the LORD lift up his countenance upon you and give you peace. (Num. 6:24–26)*

Appendix

Leading Productive Discussions

Note: This material has been adapted from curricula produced by The Bethlehem Institute (TBI), a ministry of Bethlehem Baptist Church. It is used by permission.

I t is our conviction that the best group leaders foster an environment in their group which engages the participants. Most people learn by solving problems or by working through things that provoke curiosity or concern. Therefore, we discourage you from ever "lecturing" for the entire lesson. Although a group leader will constantly shape conversation, clarifying and correcting as needed, they will probably not talk for the majority of the lesson. This study guide is meant to facilitate an investigation into biblical truth—an investigation that is shared by the group leader and the participants. Therefore, we encourage you to adopt the posture of a "fellow-learner" who invites participation from everyone in the group.

It might surprise you how eager people can be to share what they have learned in preparing for each lesson. Therefore, you should invite participation by asking your group participants to share their discoveries. Here are some of our "tips" on facilitating discussion that is engaging and helpful:

- Don't be uncomfortable with silence initially. Once the first participant shares their response, others will be likely to join in. But if you cut the silence short by prompting them, then they are more likely to wait for you to prompt them every time.

- Affirm every answer, if possible, and draw out the participants by asking for clarification. Your aim is to make them feel comfortable sharing their ideas and learning, so be extremely hesitant to "shut down" a group member's contribution or "trump" it with your own. This does not mean, however, that you shouldn't correct false ideas—just do it in a spirit of gentleness and love.

- Don't allow a single person, or group of persons, to dominate the discussion. Involve everyone, if possible, and intentionally invite participation from those who are more reserved or hesitant.

- Labor to show the significance of their study. Emphasize the things that the participants could not have learned without doing the homework.

- Avoid talking too much. The group leader should not monopolize the discussion, but rather guide and shape it. If the group leader does the majority of the talking, the participants will be less likely to interact and engage, and therefore they will not learn as much. Avoid constantly adding the "definitive last word."

- The group leader should feel the freedom to linger on a topic or question if the group demonstrates interest. The group leader should also pursue digressions that are helpful and relevant. There is a balance to this, however: the group leader *should* attempt to cover the material. So avoid the extreme of constantly wandering off topic, but also avoid the extreme of limiting the conversation in a way that squelches curiosity or learning.

- The group leader's passion, or lack of it, is infectious. Therefore, if you demonstrate little enthusiasm for the material, it is almost inevitable that your participants will likewise be bored. But if you have a genuine excitement for what you are studying, and if you truly think Bible study is worthwhile, then your group will be impacted positively. Therefore, it is our recommendation that before you come to the group, you spend enough time working through the homework and praying, so that you can overflow with genuine enthusiasm for the Bible and for God in your group. This point cannot be stressed enough. Delight yourself in God and in his Word!